W9-CIQ-501

# Prayers To Pray
## wherever you are

*Also by Jeanette Struchen*

PRAYERS TO PRAY WITHOUT REALLY TRYING

# Prayers To Pray wherever you are

by
Jeanette Struchen



J. B. LIPPINCOTT COMPANY
*Philadelphia & New York*

First edition

Printed in the United States of America

Library of Congress Catalog Card Number: 69-14498

*To my parents*

# Introduction

Most of us live life on a griddle.
We eat on the run, sleep during commercials, and stand on our heads trying to find out what it's all about.

The faster we go, the more we need a few unshakables in religious faith. They need to be simple, honest, and workable. The rest we should throw over a shoulder to dangle loosely in the winds of change.

Man does not live by faith alone, but it is my hope that the following pieces may fit into the reader's personal jigsaw puzzle of spiritual growth.

*Jeanette Struchen*

*God,* help me pray it like it is.

In the midst of explosion people cry, scream, and pray
without stalling for proper words
or
acceptable posture.

The world is exploding, Lord,
with change and crises,
with hate and cruelty,
with pain and fear,
with money and prejudice,
with potential and obligation.
But man's hide is toughened against change and numb to
vicarious pain.

Don't embalm him as he is, Lord.
Show him how to crack the escape hatch through prayer.

*Amen*

*Most of us* are flesh, bone, and a hank of inconsistencies.
We pay high prices for tangibles and expect the
intangibles free.
All our lives we work at getting the budget balanced
between value and cost, quality and need
and never give a thought to the price of faith.

Faith costs.

It may cost prestige, a higher level of living, friends,
admission of error or even money.
It may cost a higher grade during exams, loss of business,
acceptance into a club or a vote.
It may cost our lives.

The cost of faith is propped on two legs–the intensity of
our convictions
and our understanding of discipleship.

*Our town* has scooped up all its concern, Lord,
and
its tokenism.
We nailed down a youth program, swept the jails,
drummed up jobs for a few oldsters, and met
the community chest goal.
But we struck out on school integration
and
Our fair housing dreams crumbled like crackers in a box.
Rent is going up here. It's costing me more time, more
responsibility, more pressure, and more headaches.
If this is a second American Revolution, Lord, it's
a lot harder than dumping tea.

*Amen*

*Doubts* are not chains designed to shackle faith.
They are healthy promptings to inner research.

Doubts are not danger signs warning of thin ice in faith.
They are directional signs pointing the way to a safer area.

Take doubts seriously. It may be honest confession of them will lead to stronger affirmations of faith.

*Hey there,* is anybody listening?
Can I be saved?

There hasn't been an idea in my head for a month of
    Sundays or a lick of interest in anything.
What's all this for, anyhow–work, sleep, eat, walk, talk,
    wish?
If this is a shakedown in preparation for
    another world,
    forget it–I've had it right here.
Do you know I've worked all week, cleaned my
    apartment and watched TV every night–except
    when I sat on that park bench watching a squirrel
    who sat watching me.
Alcohol is too expensive, hobbies are too boring, people
    are too frightening, sex is too temporary and pot is
    too risky.
        So what's left? And don't tell me religion!
That's for the insecure, and after all I'm not insecure.
        Am I?
    Am I insecure?
    Is anybody listening?

*Amen*

*Love* washes the strain out of life.
Love makes us new and whole.
Love compels faith.
Love lifts faith.
Love supports faith.
Love becomes energy for good.
Love is unselfish.
Love jumps barriers of skin color.
Love ignores zones of silence between nations.
Love is eager.
Love is patient.
Love penetrates walls that split man from his brother.
Love is not egotistical.
Love tears prejudice into shreds and absorbs selfishness
into streams of purpose.

*Pass* the loving cup, Lord.

Now that we've carved out the bush and wired the world
for sound, we are struggling over what to say.
We have shot the moon with film and scratched its face
with a minishovel and ask what else is new to do.
We have rolled out freeways across a million pastures
and in boredom ask where is there to go?

Father, I know man cannot live by inventions alone, and
after the noisy gong and clanging cymbals of
progress have passed, let there be love–let there be
love–let there be love.

*Amen*

"*Who* made the world?"

"God. God made everything."

"God didn't make my house; carpenters did."

"Yeah, but God made the carpenters. God made all things that are alive. He made our apple tree, and the ladybug in this box, and us–and He knows what we're doin' all the time. . .even when we have secrets, He knows the secrets."

"Aw, He doesn't."

"Yes, He does. We're all God's children."

"Well, my mom doesn't know my secrets, and I'm her children."

"You mean you're her child."

"Well, she still doesn't know my secrets."

Faith comes from everybody we ever met, every book we ever read, every heartache, every pain, and every shining moment. Faith is our greatest compilation of scattered ideas, courageous moments and noble thoughts.

*Father,* did you know a star dropped tonight?
I saw it go quickly as a tear slides down a cheek
    and drops from sight–and as noiselessly.
It fell with a flourish, Lord.
Was it going somewhere special
    or just changing positions
    to get a better perspective on the Universe?

*Amen*

*Not all* the pills, clubs, games, television, or people
themselves can dent loneliness like religious faith.
Faith is a frightened soldier humming, a frantic mother
praying, a dying patient believing.
Faith is not more complicated today than in ages past
but the demands upon man are more complicated.
The world is more complicated. Society is more
complicated. Complications keep rocking the boat.

*That picnic* was a real happening, Lord.
Did the person who arranged the lie-in between courses
also pour vodka in the watermelons?
Without three-legged races and softball is the only
alternative pinning doilies on blown-up pictures
of models?
You can tell, Lord, it has been a long time since I
went on a picnic. In the interim not only have fun
and games changed their make-up but morals have
changed their shape.

Society is one big rumpus room.

*Amen*

*To keep* the record straight, it is only fair to say that
God does not purposely, with malice, send us
obstacles. No loving father puts obstacles in the
path of his children even to test their endurance.
When obstacles are there, however, a wise father
uses them as a learning experience whereby the
child may grow. So it must be with God.
If we believe that God is–more than this, if we
believe that God is good, totally good, all-the-time
good–we know He does not change His nature to
maliciously put obstacles in the path
of His children.

*How* could I know she was pregnant, Lord?
All I knew was that she cut classes, failed tests,
ignored homework, and concocted excuses.
The whole time she was looking for a cheap abortionist.

Forgive me for my inability to read the secret burden
of a fifteen-year-old.

*Amen*

*Do we* have to endure pain to appreciate health? No. But after pain comes a richness that cannot be described or experienced in any other way. All the way through the agony of pain is the opportunity for either bitterness or a strange and wonderful inner strengthening. No one can substitute for us at such a time.

*O God,* it's malignant!

I'm so afraid.
The very word scares me.

He promised to tell me, and now I'm sorry he did. No, I
don't mean that.
I'm thankful he told me.
Shall I tell Jack and the kids? How shall I tell them?
What about the kids, Lord?
They need me healthy and strong.
And all the time I thought I was indispensable.
What does malignant mean? An
operation–treatment–recovery–or does it mean
something I can't even think about?

Make me strong, Lord.
If I can't beat it with medicine, make me strong enough
to bear it with dignity.

O God, pardon my tears. They are for all the unknowns
ahead.

*Amen*

*Prayer* is not only faith affirmed; it is faith in action.

It is doing something when there seems to be nothing else to do. It is an action where no action seems possible. Sometimes it is an involuntary and even instinctual awareness of an Other, of One who is there, who hears, who can respond, who may respond. The very act of praying instills faith because it is faith expressed beyond mental contemplation into a leap of dependence. If prayer is this significant in moments of emergency, then the cultivation of a life of prayer is the cultivation of faith as surely as one plants a seed, waters, and feeds it.

*O Lord,* it's hard to be invisible.

I've got a sheepskin, a good job, and money.
But I've also got a black face.
"The house is not for sale." That means he took it
off the market until I get off the porch.
"Another offer pending" means it's pending in his
mind as long as I'm standing there.

Lord, who hooked America on red, white, and blue
when its charter members were
red, white, and black?

I've made myself decent, law-abiding, and loving.
Now if I could only make myself white and break
out of slavery.

*Amen*

*Of all* the gifts ever given, of all boxes handled and
untied, of all thanks expressed, of all happiness
shared over an act of giving, one gift stands alone.
A gift given in sheer love. A gift too priceless to
be enclosed in a fancy box. It had to be encased
within the crowning receptacle
of all creation–man.

The gift is God's love within us.

So precious the gift. So beholden the recipient.

*O God,* are you down here with these winos?

They've lost track of you. They've lost track of
humanity too.
In fact, they've lost track of every decent idea they
ever had and galvanized their weaknesses
with the bottle.
Maybe some of them lived in the eye of a tornado at
home and couldn't take it.
Maybe some copped out on strangling responsibilities.
But they're sick, Lord—weak and sick men
who couldn't say "NO."
So they've chosen hell in a flophouse.
Don't you drop them, Lord, as the rest of us have.

*Amen*

*Ideas* punch holes in the dark and let in light and fresh air. Both light and air are essential to growth. But it takes personal will to keep reading books with hefty ideas. Our culture is full of invitations to escape. We cannot forget that ideas brought man out of the cave.

When we grow mentally, we are jacking up our fortifications to meet life. We are structuring girders to support useful thoughts. Consciously and unconsciously we are shoring up weak foundations with something more durable.

*O God,* thank you for creating this big brown dog
stretched beside me.
For placing the clock in his stomach which prods my
forgetfulness,
For his careful listening ability without offering
advice,
For his instinct in making his moods match mine,
For his ability to take me as I am, not requiring more,
For answering my invitational whistle for
companionship,
For steering clear when I am preoccupied,
For forgiving me after five days in a kennel,
For guarding my property when I am away,
For barking when strangers approach the children.

Thank you, Lord, for your special gift to man by
creating dogs.

*Amen*

*Prayer* is not outmoded. We do not outgrow it.
Prayer is for people with knowledge–with such knowledge that they have caught a glimmer of their own finiteness.
Prayer is for the strong-willed, the impatient and the demanding people. It is a force stronger than their own. It absorbs their resoluteness and refocuses it.
Prayer is for people with such talent that they see their own shortcomings and begin to remeasure themselves.
Prayer is a cry for help, an arm for steadiness, a hand for guidance.
Prayer is the receptacle for sin, the letter pleading for forgiveness, the free breath of confession.
Prayer is a basket of nourishment, a nest of security, a walk in the woods of doubt.

*What* is he preaching, Lord?

That I pray better in church than anyplace else?
        I can't buy that!
What about that day in the subway when the old man
        fell and I was the only one around
            or
        the prayer from the draft board office when the
            guy reclassified Bobbie?
Remember the day I prayed for overtime
        when the rent was due
        and at the hospital
        when the baby lived through the night?
O God, that's prayin'–believe me–
        that's real prayin', Lord.

*Amen*

*In prayer,* expect dry periods and expect to wait for answers.

Our dearest friends are not always bubbling over in our presence, nor do they offer ready answers and advice on all our problems. In fact, they may be quite reticent to offer advice at all, and we respect them for it. This does not mean they do not love us. It does not mean they do not have answers. The God who listens when we pray may seem to act much the same. Guidance is not poured into us. Answers do not come as though God were a celestial genie waiting to respond to our instant bidding.

*Life* takes a lot of patience, Lord. . . .
Children wait to become adults,
The sick wait for health,
Employees wait for vacations,
Investors wait for high dividends,
Farmers wait for bountiful crops,
Prisoners wait for freedom,
The sleepless wait for morning,
Fishermen wait for lucky strikes,
Actors wait for the big break.
We ask, like the Psalmist, Lord, "How long?"

OH!
Until we learn that waiting is part of the whole plan.

*Amen*

*A* serious college senior sat before me ready to spread
out his theological doubts.

"I cannot believe in God. Man is adequate without
all this otherworldliness."
"Do you ever pray?" I asked.
"Sure, once in a while. I suppose most people do."
"Who listens?"

We can believe in God and not pray, but we
cannot pray disbelieving in God.

*O God,* what does it mean to be a good citizen?
To march for war and jeopardize the peace
or
march for peace and jeopardize the war?
To salute flags and cork-up sentiment over people
or
salute people and cork-up sentiment over flags?
To collide with the establishment and shout for change
or
collide with change and shout for the
establishment?

In such an age forgive us, Lord, if we're up tight over
the meaning of citizenship.

*Amen*

*Faith* grows in fits and starts.

As children and youth we learn so much within a few short years that when we hit middle-age-drag, it is easy to forget that the growing edge was given for lifetime use.

Faith may grow early and fast or late and slow. It may grow shapeless or be shaped by creeds and doctrines. It may grow wide and inclusive or narrow and exclusive. There is not a solitary pattern.

*Some* parents aren't people, Lord!

It is disquieting to me when
a mother offers her daughter The Pill to maintain
family honor,
a dad gives a rifle "To Johnny with love" when
Johnny totes a reputation for hot temper and
irresponsibility,
parents foot the booze bill for an after-graduation
blast or
laugh when Junior maneuvers the police out of a
speeding fine.

When the meek inherit the earth, Lord, they may have
more on their hands than they bargained for.

*Amen*

*One* summer morning Henry was boarding the bus for retarded children's camp, and his mind and body slipped over into a seizure. The alert camp director, with great compassion, put his arm around Henry's shoulders. For several minutes they sat on the front seat of the bus. . .Henry in another world and the director watching for signs of re-entry.

The sign came. Henry snapped back. Unable to speak but with slowly stretching smile, he turned to the director as if to say, "Thank you for loving me through my illness."

So it is with a loving Father. Some people find Him quite naturally through illness. Others are led hopelessly to the thin edges of atheism. Then, through desperate fear, sheer guilt, or careful guidance they are pulled away from the precipice.

In illness, faith is the power in patience. It is the healer without pills. It is the courage without words and voices.

*That mother* has the patience of an oak tree, Lord.
Her little boy can't talk or hear or think and still
she strains to translate his gurgling and treat him
as a normal boy.
She wouldn't want stars in a crown, Lord, for all her
patient outpouring. I doubt she would want
anything at all
except to witness a miracle for her child.
Somewhere in the great tomorrow I pray, O God,
that you will unstop his ears
and give him a great thought to call his own.

And thank you, Lord, for showing me Job's patience
at work in today's world.

*Amen*

*There* is a story told about Bishop Quayle, who had been under stress from a personal problem. He said, "I thought I heard God's voice saying, 'Quayle, you go to bed; I'll sit up all night.' "

To have faith that Someone is there; to have faith that individual life is valuable and not an accident; to believe that a plan is being worked out over millenniums, and order and goodness are a part of it; to believe that God loves us in spite of our self-pity, jealousies, and petty egos; to believe that Someone listens when we pray and can bring something worth while out of our mistakes; this is to have faith in a personal God. It is to say, "Somebody is there!"

*They* wouldn't even answer the door.
I knocked a dozen times, Lord, and heard their raucous
laugh muffle into stark silence.
All I needed was a telephone. Why didn't they open up?
Between slats in the blinds I could see people at a
card table. They were four, and I was one.
In sheets of rain it was my fifth attempt at a lighted
house, but nobody answers doors any more after
dark. No telling how far a garage was, and the car
konked out two blocks back.
I pounded harder, trying to shake water from my clothes.
"Go away," a voice called.
"I need help!"
"He doesn't live here."
"Could you call a garage for me?"
Silence. Then through a locked door.
"It'll be twenty minutes."

Lord, do you know how hard it is to find a Samaritan?

*Amen*

*If* heaven is an island, most of us sail around and lightly touch shore once in a while. A few get out and hike around. Nobody makes permanent camp. But to deny the existence of such a spot, even as a condition of the spirit, is to nail down a lid on life.

Spiritual renewal is like touching a corner of the island of heaven. We drift into shore with empty cups—sometimes chipped and broken with the shine rubbed off. We ride out on a crest of new energy.

What is spiritual renewal?

It is an opening of heart and mind,
letting the winds of holiness
blow through the musty nooks.

It is discovery of a new dimension of existence—
as the baby bird discovers on first flight.

It is unplugged relief when the dragons of
imagination lose their fire and drop their tails.

It is relaxing of the armored guard around
the picket fence of pride.

It is energy in the lifeline of faith.

*How* can we still be friends, Lord?
I've owed her a letter for six months, and she keeps on
writing. What is it with loyalty? She forgives my
negligence, pardons my excuses, and encourages
the activities which strap my time.
When I call her long distance, she spends three minutes
telling me I shouldn't be so extravagant.
By the time my "sorry I missed your birthday" card
reaches her, she laughingly applies it to next year
and commends my efficiency for being
a year ahead.
Dear God, bless with special favor the long-suffering
friends who take us as we are and still love us.

*Amen*

*Just* as faith has not come without cost, neither has it come without debt. All that we are, all that we believe, all that we know, we owe to someone.

Our grasp upon the future can never exceed our debt to the past. No one of us is free from his inheritance in the ancient drawings on caves and mysterious scratches on rocks.

*Do* I have to listen to all that garbage from him again
today, Lord?
That boy must have a pinched nerve in his head. Nobody
believes him. Nobody trusts him. He has more
excuses than a weatherman and knows more
cracked pots than a florist.
Who taught him to lie like that, and where did he pick
up the squadron of devils that fly around inside
him?
It isn't his long hair–it's his attitude.
He is flip and sassy. He is brash and sneaky.
I'm afraid to turn my other cheek for fear he'll knock
me down. How can I teach him arithmetic, Lord,
when he doesn't even want to be a human being?

*Amen*

*By law* we are required to take an annual accounting of
our material possessions. We may spend several
days figuring out what happened to pay checks,
how much we gave away, and how much we owe.
To do the same with our faith may not be as exacting
but is surely as profitable.

*Father,* thank you for letting Christmas be more
than a bright star, an angel's song, and a gold vase.

Help me remember:
There were labor pains, a crying baby, a dirty shed,
and a loud party in a crowded inn.
When there were such pain and poverty and need
heralding the Prince of Peace, how did we get hung
up on angels?

*Amen*

*When* Jesus called the twelve, he did not hand them a book on faith. He called them to follow and grow. He called them into a new awareness of life and to a wide-eyed view of people. The disciples asked questions. They may even have winked at a few ideas and turned thumbs down on others. These men were real. Peter's urgent cry in the storm, "Lord, save me," is as old as man himself. Life is flooded by surprise storms. Something is always rocking the boat. We recognize it. We spend our lives adjusting to the motions, plugging holes, and keeping on course.

*Man* needs a fuzzy security blanket, Lord.
He jumps to answer social alarms and rushes out
to fight only the smoke.
He shakes the goosebumps out of the national anthem
but refuses to shake the glory out of war.
He gasps over world hunger but refuses to go on a diet.
He makes stabs at humanizing his community but winds
up homogenizing it.

O God, man cannot live by security alone, but let's
begin again with the blanket.

*Amen*

*We* can be blindfolded and not see it, leave town and hope to escape it, close our minds and ignore it, but change is inevitable. Mankind decides whether to mount it courageously and direct its course, or let it stampede the corral. Man can change the course of rivers, irrigate deserts, split mountains, shoot the moon and calm his jitters by pills. But he is timid in transition, and shaky in morality. His greatest danger must not be fear of change, but fear of apathy and an anemic sense of responsibility.

*The church* is dropping its old skin, Lord.
Have you noticed?
It had grown flabby from guarding its treasure
    instead of healthy from running to give it away.
Please allow it to hang loose until it's free from
    growing pains and help us realize that before
    it can be frisky in the fields of service, Lord,
    it has to be free of its old skin.

*Amen*

*When* the mind wanders in prayer, try again.
When the telephone interrupts prayer, try again after
the conversation.
When sleep conquers prayer, start where you left
off upon awaking.
Hard? Yes!
So was balancing a bike on the first try, but after each
fall stark perseverance kept us at it until
riding was relaxed enjoyment.

*We're back* at paying lip service to the rules, Lord.
Talk is cheaper than air and as polluted.
Today the world feels like a stuffy closet
    where people come vacuum-packed in high-risers.
    The world must have been beautiful
    before man made it crowded
    and peaceful before man made it violent.

Lord, is there an alternative to canned living?

*Amen*

*Prayer* is dangerous.

If we persist, we may be robbed of some of our fondest possessions. Our egos might be stolen never to be recovered. Our self-pity could disappear, and jealousies might take wing never to be found.

More than these, however, is the danger in praying, "Thy will be done." God's full answer to such a petition might not be to our liking. It might be revolutionary. What if it meant leaving the present job and going to an overseas mission station? What if it meant separating from a social group which brings enjoyment? What if it meant going out on a limb at work in order to stand up for convictions? What if it meant restraining some old habits or cutting off a friendship?

To pray is to expect change: change in ourselves, in a situation, in a condition. The change may not be our wish for ourselves, but it may be His will for us.

*Why* doesn't somebody wait on me, Lord?
I've stood here for ten minutes.
One clerk is on coffee break, two are at lunch, and
this one is a pinch hitter about to strike out.
Why is the world so technically smooth
and humanly rocky?
My charge plate is right, the cash register works,
and the scales are accurate.
But the clerk is tired and grumpy. She broke her pencil
and has mislaid the sales slip.

Lord, the whole curriculum of creation seems fine
and dandy until it comes to people.
Should you recheck the recipe?

*Amen*

*Any* miracles from God today?

Did not light come out of total darkness into the room this morning? Did something new spring up in the yard when you were not looking? Is there breath within your body without your giving it a second thought? Did something wonderful slip into your mind that happened yesterday or a dozen years ago?

Then you are the recipient of some wonderful Power who seems to care and loves you enough to bestow such miracles.

*That guy* is for real, Lord.
He likes people first–not rules, schedules, perfection,
and THEN people.
He's bright, Lord, with a sixth sense about an employee
who is in hock up to the eyebrows
or one full of nitty-gritty complaints
about the office.
He can tag them every time.
I've seen him burned up, mocked out, dog tired,
and ripsnorting with fun.
But I've never seen him petty, unjust, insincere,
or impatient.
Whatever keeps him going is more than daily vitamins.
When work is heavy, he holes up behind closed doors.
When it's light, he falls in with the rest of us and
then heads out to play nine holes.
Thanks, Lord, for creating special people who love their
job, let it show, and allow their joy to rub off
on the rest of us.

*Amen*

*Grief* may paralyze faith and separate us from God.
Grief is the bulldozer against life's fragileness. It is the thief who steals away joy. It is the stark soberer–the mysterious puzzler.
Grief cannot be cured by sympathy cards or a cheering up. It can only be redirected to something as forceful but forceful-positive.

While held in the clutches of grief, a captive feels seized and marooned on a solitary island. It is difficult to communicate. It is difficult to believe anyone else has ever been in the same detached spot. It is difficult to hope the situation will ever end. For some it is a time of groping, or straying away religiously. For others it is a time of spiritual renewal.
Those who have strong investments in religious faith can be as seaworthy through grief as they are in the experience of life. The boat keeps rocking, but it is deeply anchored.

*They died* last night, Lord, not physically but morally.
I saw them leave together in a fit of booze and laughter.
Carefree, they smacked conformity in the face
　　and took off.
Why didn't they think of tomorrow, Lord?

Live excuses are as hard to resurrect
　　as understanding spouses.
It might have helped if they had taken time to zoom in
　　and get focused on the situation–or if they had
　　prayed, "Lead us not into temptation."
The weakness is, Lord, they heard society cooing its
　　pardon, "Forgive those who trespass
　　against us."

*Amen*

*Every* occasion for decision-making is
an opportunity for growing.
David made a courageous decision against odds
when all he had was a slingshot, a few pebbles,
a terrific aim, and his faith.
Saint Paul had to face a choice, after the light left
him on the Damascus road, as to what
he would do with his life.
The disciples were never coerced into following
Jesus. Several times they must have heard him say,
"If a man would follow. . ."
There was always the possibility of dropouts.

*Why* should I dye my hair blonde, Lord?
I have enough trouble as it is.
Next year the swing will be back to brunettes, so
I'll sit this one out.
I don't know who decided blondes have more fun,
but it wasn't a blonde.
Nobody thinks of himself as having the most fun. Fun
is always more so on the other side of the fence.
My guess is that the manufacturers of super-lashes never
wore them. Who needs to see the world through
mink except minks?
Neither did a serious swimmer invent the bikini
or a female public speaker the miniskirt.

People are funny, Lord.
Did you create them out of whim or fatal flaw?

*Amen*

*We* collect charity by the basket for those who have nothing to eat but crumbs. In faith even crumbs have substance. They have been touched by leaven from the whole loaf, and a crumb of faith may be like light at the end of a tunnel to one having a spiritual blackout.

*Keep us* from being the spitting image of another
generation, Lord.
Help us to stand up, sit down, pitch in, be in,
tune in, and make a dent in
this overstacked, split-up, hung-up world.
Allow us to explode the myths, shake the ideals,
spring the traps, can the fakes, tame the systems,
and start a healthy pulse beat
toward the levitation of society.

*Amen*

*Surprised* by an oriole!
How much better than by a wrapped-up gift.
Lord, how long had he watched before whistling?
He caught me unawares.
Was he sharing an idea
or
Giving me instructions for the day?
He wasn't scolding, Lord–just whistlin' happy.
He lifted the latch on winter and left me spring.

*Amen*